MW01493869

PUFFY

www.thepuffystory.com

⊙ @thepuffystory

ⓕ @thepuffystory

To all the little girls in this world, may your imagination soar like the wind and your joy shine bright like the sun.
We love you.

Hi! My name is Puffy, and I live on Kayla's head.

Living on Kayla's head can be a lot of fun,
but sometimes it can get a little crazy.

Let me tell you about the time when I was an angry grumpy puff.

A lot of times Kayla and Mommy would pull and tug me.

Sometimes I went left.

Sometimes I went right.

Even up and down!

Sometimes this even made me lose my friends.

One afternoon, I remember being so thirsty and hungry that I shriveled up!!

All of this made me quite angry.

I mean, sheesh! I tried to cooperate, I promise I did, but Kayla just didn't get it. So I decided to do something that I knew would get Kayla's attention...

I caused a
BAD HAIR
DAY!

Strand by strand, I squeezed myself out of the hair scrunchy and threw all of my arms and legs around Kayla's head!

Hello!!!

Kayla looked up at me and tried to make me
feel better.
She tried to tickle me, but
that wasn't going to work.

I was still an angry grumpy puff.

Kayla noticed that it was raining outside and decided to take me for a walk to blow off some steam.

She knew how much fun we always had in the rain. We danced. We sang. We even tried to drink the rain!

As the rain continued to pour, I couldn't help but smile.
I was no longer an angry grumpy puff. My best friend
Kayla knew just what to do.

So I opened my mouth and drank as much rain as I could!

Mmm! Delicious!

All of a sudden, in mid gulp, the clouds opened up!

Out flew a Fairy Hair Mother with wings the color of gold glitter dazzling in the sun. Her hair flowed down her back like waves in the ocean and her gown was my favorite color, green!! She even had a crown on her head!!

She was beautiful.

Kayla and I looked in awe.

She slowly flew over to us and whispered that she had a secret!

"Hi Kayla. Hi Puffy. I'm your fairy hair mother. I have this magical hair oil for you. One drop is all you need to make your Puffy smile indeed."

Kayla agreed and squeezed a drop of oil into her hand and started rubbing it all over me.

"Haha haha haha. That tickles, Kayla!"

I was soo happy. I could hardly contain myself. I could stretch and I could bounce. I loved this oil!

The Fairy Hair Mother giggled and flew away, but not before leaving a glittery golden bottle of magical hair oil in Kayla's hands.

Ahh that was such a good day! I will never forget it.

Now every night before we go to sleep, Kayla lathers me in the magical oil.

I wake up feeling fluffy and happy!

I am no longer an angry grumpy puff.

"I love you Kayla!"

"I love you Puffy!"

Kelechi Onyejiaka and Nastasha Pollard met at the University of Miami and have been best friends for over 10 years. They share a love for traveling, investing, cycling, trying new foods, and story telling. They are passionate about their stories celebrating diversity and providing young girls with characters that are a reflection of themselves. Nastasha currently resides in New York City working as a Certified Registered Nurse Anesthetist providing Anesthesia at a large teaching hospital and an ambulatory surgery center. Kelechi currently resides in Philadelphia working on her dream of becoming a world renowned dentist and running an online tutoring business.